This edition published by Parragon Books Ltd in 2015

Parragon Books Ltd
Chartist House
15–17 Trim Street
Bath BA1 1HA, UK
www.parragon.com

Written by Clement C. Moore   Edited by Lily Holland
Illustrated by Harriet Muncaster   Designed by Ailsa Cullen
Production by Marina Blackburn

ISBN 978-1-4748-2027-1

Printed in China

For
Grandpa and Granny
H. M.

The Night Before
Christmas

Clement C. Moore
Harriet Muncaster

Bath · New York · Cologne · Melbourne · Delhi
Hong Kong · Shenzhen · Singapore · Amsterdam

'Twas the night before Christmas,
when all through the house
Not a creature was stirring,
not even a mouse.

The stockings were hung
by the chimney with care,
In hope that St Nicholas
soon would be there.

The children were nestled all snug in their beds,
While visions of sugarplums danced in their heads.

And Mama in her 'kerchief
and I in my cap,
Had just settled down for a
long winter's nap.

When out on the lawn there
arose such a clatter,
I sprang from my bed to see what
was the matter.

Away to the window
I flew like a flash,
Tore open the shutters and
threw up the sash.

The moon on the breast of
the new-fallen snow
Gave lustre of midday to
objects below,

When, what to my wondering eyes should appear,
But a miniature sleigh and eight tiny reindeer.
With a little old driver so lively and quick,
I knew in a moment it must be St Nick.

More rapid than eagles his coursers they came,
And he whistled and shouted and called
them by name;

"Now Dasher! Now Dancer! Now Prancer and Vixen!
On Comet! On Cupid! On Donner and Blitzen!

"To the top of the porch! To the top of the wall!
Now dash away! Dash away! Dash away all!"

As dry leaves that before
the wild hurricane fly,
When they meet with an obstacle,
mount to the sky,

So up to the housetop
the coursers they flew,
With a sleigh full of toys
and St Nicholas too.

And then in a twinkling,
I heard on the roof
The prancing and pawing
of each little hoof.

As I drew in my head,
and was turning around,
Down the chimney St Nicholas
came with a bound.

He was dressed all in fur,
from his head to his foot,
And his clothes were all tarnished
with ashes and soot.

A bundle of toys he had flung on his back,
And he looked like a pedlar
just opening his pack.

His eyes – how they twinkled!
His dimples – how merry!
His cheeks were like roses, his nose like a cherry!
His droll little mouth was drawn up like a bow,
And the beard of his chin was as white as the snow.

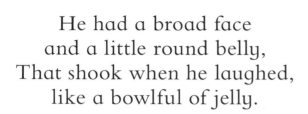

He had a broad face
and a little round belly,
That shook when he laughed,
like a bowlful of jelly.

He was chubby and plump,
a right jolly old elf,
And I laughed when I saw him,
in spite of myself.

A wink of his eye
and a twist of his head,
Soon gave me to know
I had nothing to dread.

He spoke not a word,
but went straight to his work,
And filled all the stockings,
then turned with a jerk,

And laying his finger
aside of his nose
And giving a nod,
up the chimney he rose.

He sprang to his sleigh,
to his team gave a whistle,
And away they all flew
like the down of a thistle.

But I heard him exclaim
ere he drove out of sight,

"Merry Christmas to all, and to all a goodnight!"